Content

. . . .

What is the red planet? 2
The first trip to Mars 4
Mariner 9 6
The first probes to land on Mars . . 8
A robot car on Mars 10
Craters and mountains 14
Rocks, dust and soil 16
Pictures of Mars 18
Mars fact-file 20
Index 24

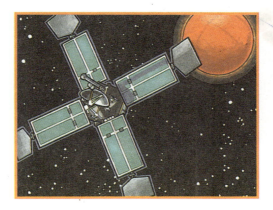

What is the red planet?

We live on Earth. Earth is a planet. It orbits the sun. To orbit means to go around.

Mars is a planet, too. It glows red in the sky. It is called the red planet.

Mars orbits the same sun as Earth. It is 228 million kilometres from the sun.

The planets orbit the sun.

The first trip to Mars

The first trip to Mars was made by a space probe. It was in 1964. The space probe was called Mariner 4.

Mariner 4 was carried into space by a rocket. Mariner 4 took seven and a half months to get to Mars. It did not land on the planet.

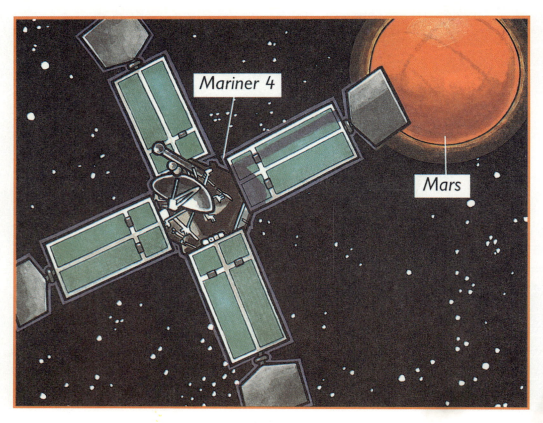

Mariner 4 did not land on the planet Mars.

Mariner 4 was carried into space by a rocket.

Mariner 9

The first space probe to orbit Mars was Mariner 9. It went to Mars in 1971.

Mariner 9 took five and a half months to get to Mars. It did not land on Mars.

Mariner 9 orbits Mars.

The first probes to land on Mars

In 1975 two space probes went on a trip to Mars. These probes were called Viking 1 and Viking 2. They were the first probes to land on Mars.

Viking 1 took ten months to get to Mars. It took pictures of the planet.

Viking 2 took eleven months to get to Mars.

This is a picture that Viking 1 took of Mars.

A robot car on Mars

In 1997 another space probe went on a trip to Mars. This space probe was called Pathfinder. It took seven months to get to Mars. Pathfinder landed on the planet.

This is the space probe called Pathfinder.

Pathfinder landed on Mars.

Pathfinder had a robot car on it. The robot car was called a rover. The rover drove slowly over Mars. It drove slowly for 84 days.

This is the rover robot car.

The rover drove slowly over Mars.

Craters and mountains

We have found out a lot on our trips to Mars. In 1965 we found out that Mars had deep craters. We did not know what had made the craters.

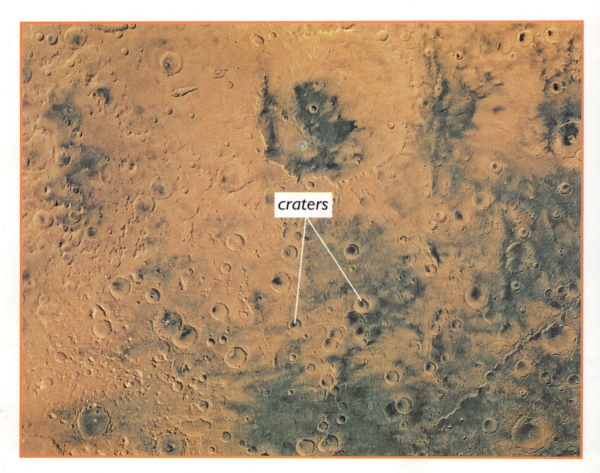

These are the craters on Mars.

In 1971 we found out that Mars had a big volcano. The volcano is 26 400 metres high. It is three times higher than the highest mountain on Earth.

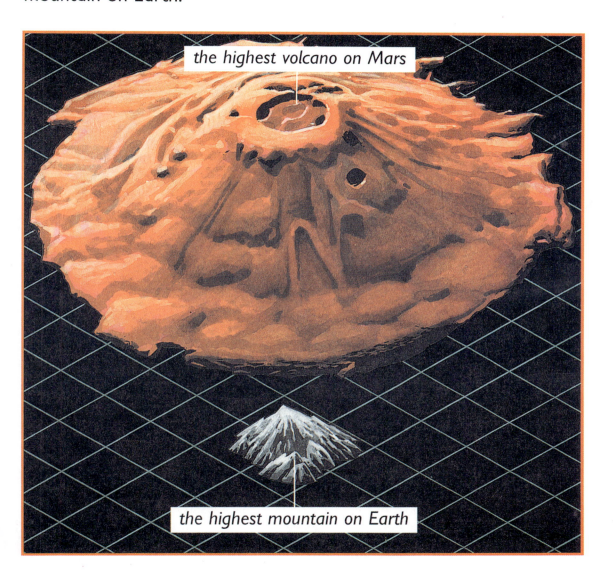

the highest volcano on Mars

the highest mountain on Earth

Rocks, dust and soil

In 1976 we found out that Mars had red rocks on it. We also found out that it had red dust on it. That is why it glows red in the sky.

The rocks, dust and soil on Mars are red.

In 1976 the Viking space probes tested the soil on Mars. We wanted to see if the soil had living things in it. No living things were found in the soil.

This Viking space probe tested the soil on Mars.

Pictures of Mars

In 1997 the rover tested the rocks on Mars. It took pictures of the rocks, too, and sent them to Earth. We found out a lot from these pictures.

The rover tested the rocks on Mars.

Mars fact-file

On our trips to Mars we have found out a lot of facts.

Fact 1

Mars is a lot colder than Earth. A very hot summer's day on Mars feels like a very cold winter's day on Earth.

Mars is a very cold planet.

Fact 2

Mars is a very windy planet. It has big dust storms. The dust storms make the sky look pink.

Mars has big dust storms.

Are these facts true or false? What do you think?
Find out at the bottom of the page.

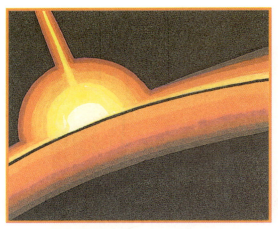

1 A day on Mars is 40 minutes longer than a day on Earth.

2 There are trees on Mars today.

3 There is ice on Mars.

4 We can breathe the air on Mars.

What will we find out about the red planet on our next trip to Mars?
Watch this space!

Index

C
craters 14

D
dust 16, 21

E
Earth 2, 3, 15, 20, 22

O
orbit 2, 3, 6

P
planet 2, 3, 4, 9,
10, 20, 21, 23

R
robot car 12, 18
rocket 4, 5
rocks 16, 18
rover 12, 18

S
sky 3, 16, 21
space probe 4, 6, 8,
10, 17
sun 2, 3

V
volcano 15

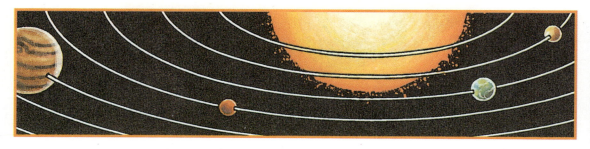